POETRY BY PETER DAVISON

PRETENDING TO BE ASLEEP

PRETENDING
TO BE
ASLEEP

POEMS BY

PETER DAVISON

ATHENEUM   NEW YORK
1970

The author is grateful to the following periodicals for permission to reprint poems that originally appeared in their pages: THE ATLANTIC; BOSTON MAGAZINE; ENCOUNTER; HARPER'S MAGAZINE; HUDSON REVIEW; KENYON REVIEW; PARTISAN REVIEW. The poems "The Pleaders" and "Making Marks" originally appeared in THE NEW YORKER. The poems "Under Protection," "The Public Garden," "The Visitant," and "Fourth Voice: The Grandmother," originally appeared in POETRY.

Thanks also to Robert Fitzgerald for lines from his translation of THE ODYSSEY, to George Seferis and his translator Rex Warner for a line from Palamos, and to Michael Maccoby for the epigraph—all to be found in "Words for my Father."

CONTENTS

I THE PLEADERS

II PRETENDING TO BE ASLEEP

III *THE YEARS*

I

THE PLEADERS

Pythagoras would say to both: What is your warrant for valuing one part of my experience and rejecting the rest? . . . If I had done so, you would never have heard my name.

F. M. CORNFORD, *The Unwritten Philosophy*

AFTER BEING AWAY

When I shall die, in body
or mind, if you survive me,
give me my due. You know
I held no certain magic
and threw no light before me.
Searching out of pain
at first, then out of habit,
and out of self at last,
I stumbled on surprises
and managed to record them.
There's only one surprise—
to be alive—and that
may be forgotten daily
if daily not remembered.
Sometimes I remembered it.

You too, my love, have watched
each day for its surprises
and touched them as they happened.
Forgive me for inflicting
my pride on your surprises
and holding to the few
that were my sole possession.

Surprise we had together
in afternoon or evening
when we were close together
or even, often, parted.
I thank you for the thousand
surprises that you gave me,
not least the gift, unhinted
and endlessly surprising,
of never being absent.

MAKING MARKS

No two conventions of teeth behave alike.
Some chatter, grip, or slash. Others strike.
Thirty-two counters measure out our breath.
What other course for words but past the teeth?
The human body holds them at its height
Better to speak with, but the worse to bite.

Teeth hold the resonance for speech and song,
Which cannot rise past tunelessness for long
Unless teeth govern them to soar and lilt—
To pierce with love, or hate up to the hilt.
Smiling, though soft in cheek, is hard in bone,
And sounds make words by trickling over stone
To give the tongue an edge to call its own.

Sounds are the stuff, yet letters are the knives
In each man's voice, the shape of what survives.
Dry bones alone can live, though fossilized
Forever. Let my words be recognized
As mine by the wear of their bite. They classify
The being that they once were brandished by
And the abrasives they were sharpened with.
This way he gnawed his life and grinned his death.

CASTAWAY

Out at sea, out of sight
of city or island, where waves
lap like tiles on a roof
reared over earth, there eyes
see nothing to see, there ears,
wave-wasted, have nothing to hear.
Only the sea of the blood
that sings forever behind
the ear and the eye, that recites
the syllables of spirit, now
makes itself heard or seen.
Old ocean parches the hide,
withers hands and fingers
and invites the drying flippers
to spread like fans, the fins
to gather into a tail,
and, smooth as a seal, the trunk
without so much as a whisper
to thrum its way to the bottom.
Only if heels, horniest
and hoofiest end of the body,
can keep their longing for land
may the mariner preserve
his true landworthiness;
kick them up, dig them in,
remembering earth to the last
where, alone, water has meaning

Earth is always most
itself at the edge of the sea
where, rising at last from the salt,
Odysseus clambered the rocks
and, drinking deep of the spring,
his muscles wracked and torn,
shielded his salt hide
with a fresh green branch, and lay
beneath its shade to sleep.

THE GUN HAND

You have been looking out for me. I held
A pistol to the ear of the Saigon captive.
It's been a busy year. I plugged the preacher
As he leaned on the lattice railing of his motel
And drilled the senator as he strode among the busboys.
I have aimed a thousand killers of all calibres
At television pictures, egg-hatted cops,
At the pulsing cartilage of a child's temple,
At the upstart cars that pass mine on the right.
I have squeezed so often you might think me weary,
But my hand is poised and clenched to squeeze again
At the next sweet target of opportunity.

THE PLEADERS

What are you going to do with us, who have
No edges, no talents, no discriminations,
Who hear no inner voices, who perceive
No visions of the future, no horizons?
We are among you; we are going to stay.

We crush, we drag, we heave, we draw the water
For you to spill. We gather together to listen
To your speeches, though your tongues run on so fast
We cannot follow, and your jokes dart in and out
Too quickly for our laughter to form itself.
We are your children, whom you treat like horses.

When crowds surge out into the streets
You have invited them; we run with them.
You give us order, speak on our behalf,
For we speak up too slowly to interrupt you.
We are the numbers ranked on your computers.
We are among you; we are going to stay.

If we knew how to pray to you, we'd pray
That you could listen long enough to listen
To what it is we think we want. We know
That what you think we want lies far away
From anything that has occurred to us.
We are your children, whom you treat like horses.

We are the eyes your eyes have never met.
We are the voice you will not wait to hear.
We are the part of you you have forgotten,
Or trampled out, or lost and wept to lose.
We are your children, whom you treat like horses.
We are among you; we are going to stay.

WHAT COUNTS

Our astronomic signallers are sure
That what they send is monitored Out There.
Whether the creatures who receive Earth's signals
Wear flesh or bone or neither, the reply
We get will be conveyed to us in numbers,
So those who man this world must be prepared
For numbers with no language. (A pulse, we call
Such signals? But that stands for blood with us.)

The words we use to amplify our numbers
Will count for little. Though they "see the stars,"
Our far communicants can send us nothing
That we have any names for—only numbers
Which in space-dialogue refer to nothing,
Not food or love, but only to themselves.
It could be heart alone that counts out there,
But without language we shall never know.

VISIONS AND VOICES

For days the television seared our eyes
with images of the many-widowed family.
We crouched to stare at their loosened faces, their fingers
on rosaries, the hunched and harnessed shoulders.
(We starve for what survival has to teach us.)
Term after term their champions had been chosen,
served, shot down, reciting Aeschylus
and Tennyson. (" 'Tis not too late to seek
a newer world," and other familiar quotations.)

Too late, as usual, the latest killing
instructs us in our love for those who seek
more than we think of seeking. Soft in our seats
we watch the people of the long procession
reeling out across the summer landscape
to hide a body shredded and cold with bullets.
No one can hold his tongue: shrilled editorials,
New Year's resolutions, blurted promises
drown out the inner yelp of unmastered hounds
who press and snuffle hungrily along
the course this body leads us. At last, at night,
his remnants vanish in the grainy ground.

Before and after death we coursed that body.
No matter if words attacked, we could shrug them off,
but his image aroused our desire and nudged our hatred.
Slogging up mountains, seized by rapids, breasting
breakers, standing stripped naked by crowds,
his body sexed us. It revealed a self
our mirrors had never included. Gawky, controlled,
athletic in action, hectoring in speech,
it performed deeds that could have broken us
and left us with the trophies of last year's hunting—
whistles, grunts and imitated animals.

"Change," his body said—but when we heard
our voices speaking, they were not our voices.
His body has emptied the screens of our sight
The people are not listening to voices.

THE ORIGIN OF SPECIES

The elements of flesh and flower
Take form in twig, in hand, in web.
Cast loose on nature's flow and ebb,
We mortals dabble for her power

And harry the shifting shapes of life
To know their truth but name our lie
With hints and handles for the eye
Like "unicorn" and "hippogriff."

Those elements of flesh and flower
Kindle new fire in cell and cell,
While, sealed within our citadel,
We name and number, curse and cower.

A WORD IN YOUR EAR
ON BEHALF OF INDIFFERENCE

History is sometimes salvaged by it, a civil servant
Who bows and smiles at weakness, at right and wrong;
At progress, poverty, peace and war; at victims,
Torture, and torturers. A skilled masseur,
Indifference smooths our faces into features
And lets our muscles work without rending each other.

Indifference-in-the-home lets tiring lovers
Share a warm bed between the defloration and
The signal for the soon-to-be-contested
Divorce to plunge both parties
In ice-water up to the arse.

Though we yell back and forth, "Let us erase our existence!"
"Let us scurry before the flailing winds of our senses!"
"Let us surrender into the hands of the forces!"
Indifference chimes in to discourage us from jumping.

My client gives us the power this side of death
To shackle ourselves, to live within our dimensions,
To ignore for hours at a time
The outrage and the dread
Of being no more than we are.

THE FORKED TONGUE

The double-dealer's house is built
With seam and scar, with stitch and patch.
His tongue invokes by sky and star
 The language of scratch.

Perjured in vocal clothes to match
His turban, surplice, or his kilt,
He tempers mind and mouth to purr
 The language of guilt.

Bicolored syntax in one quilt,
Two kinds of hate to chase and catch,
Two kinds of love: these agitate
 The language of scratch.

His brain, emboldened by the match
Of opposites, takes on a lilt
To croon whatever cadence fits
 The language of guilt.

Withdraw his hanger by its hilt
And wipe it bloodless; spring the latch;
And hear him sigh, alone, aloud,
 The language of scratch.

So crusted crime may heal and hatch
While golden syllables are spilt
To sing out false and crude and cold
 The language of guilt.

PLAUSIBLE MAN

A plausible man keeps us from feeling uneasy
by placing himself at the center of situations.
No one has ever noticed a plausible man
doing anything (or even nothing) alone.
The plausible man is ingeniously designed
to take shape with others present in his presence:
he has no scent, he cannot cast a shadow,
he leaves no ring around the bathroom tub.

In crowds, at occasions, and especially
in the presence of cameras, prominent plausible men
make their mark on film or in the notes
of observers with specialized professional training.
Their smiles may linger at the crowded banquet
beyond their departure or bloom in air not long
before they arrive; but such a smile is seldom
connected to a face which no one is watching.

The plausible man is unlikely to be found
in possession of a navel. He performs
services of course, begets statistics,
earns cash and has relations, involves himself
in affairs, and is conspicuously useful.
The plausible man has read the works about suffering
and consequently can speak of the worst without
altering the light of his eye or raising his voice.
The plans do not allow for such an implausible
outcome as dying in a room alone.

THE LOSING STRUGGLE

"Is my thought a memory, not alive?"
WALLACE STEVENS

To yield words easily gives pleasure
To the tongue that speeds their flow,
But, loosed, they linger on the surface
Like unexpected, unpenetrating rain.

Where are we to seek the words for life?
And how are we to see what must be seen
Before shaping our language to the sound of it?
What must be seen is every moment present

But hardly every moment seen. What I hear,
Like the muttering of a crowd, is seldom discerned
Although the murmur is never interrupted.
My body secretes against its rarest need.

When released, by lightning or alarum,
I can run like a deer, ravage like a lion, overhear
The creak of a mouse's toe on a wisp of straw.
Except for these times I sleep.

What are the repositories in myself
That bind me in the caverns of silence
And refuse to let me ramble at my will?
My ego stamps its foot at their refusal.

By the shore the sun embraces me.
The pleasures of water ripple through me
And take me by the singing throat.
The elms across the lake shine out like torches.

By another shore I watch the ocean scurry
Over its deeps of flounder and periwinkles,
Bearing its rockweed aloft like torches.
As its tide falls and the sandbar emerges, birds alight.

Here by the sea I cannot see as far as the mountains,
Nor do they loom over my shoulder as they once did.
Change is everything here, here everything changes,
Changes with the phases of the moon.

I have come to worship the sun, clouds, clarity,
And as deeply I distrust the moon.
I cannot bear the monthly flow of blood.
Tide and change corrupt the imagination.

I spin my fancies finer and finer,
A quota of gossamer every working day
From an old spider who does not care for flies
And webs it for the sake of the design.

My name is death. I freeze the world in light.
I see my arm, poised at my side to move,
But never moving; and my eye, my eye
Is fixed on what exists beyond existence.

AFTERWARDS

Sit down with me and rest,
    Beloved guest.
These gardens I have made
    Where summer shade
Is shaken from leaf to leaf.

Here is no desert where
    Death circles in the air.
Here the rich scent of fruit
    Has clambered from the root
To triumph on the bough.

Behind us lies the earth
    That tricked you into birth
And troubled you to death.
    Deny its names for grief
And anger now.

No longer flinch and stain
    To have it out with pain
Nor stretch your will to break
    What blood cannot forsake.
Now I have paid your debt.

I do not call you here
    To close your eyes with fear,
Despair, or counterfeit.
    Recline beneath the shade
Of gardens I have made.

II

PRETENDING TO BE ASLEEP

If a man could pass through Paradise in a dream, and have a flower presented to him as a pledge that his soul had really been there, and if he found that flower in his hand when he awoke—Ay!—and what then?

COLERIDGE: *Anima Poetae*

I. THE DESERTED POET

This part of the country is underpeopled.
Not a word waits in hiding under the ferns
To reach up for my hand and lead me out
Of myself. No words have passed this way this season:
I have forgotten even the sound of their footsteps
Whickering through the leaves at my approach.

Look at my face, never an honest one.
It covers my desertion by pretending
That words have never meant a thing to me.
This face settles for the lie. It puts on
Creases of feigned anger between the eyes,
Furrows of mock surprise across the brow.

I wear the mask of an actor who returns
From a long journey to find his wife and children dead.

II. IN THE DOCK

Tried by the day, I stand condemned at night.
The evidence of years of fraud and shame
Waits until darkness to be brought to light.
Crime hangs from every letter of my name.

Each day conceals its treachery and blight
In places no defendant could disclaim:
Beneath the shirt, the mattress, out of sight
Behind the portrait smiling from its frame.

Night comes to sentence me. My second sight
Fixes me steadily within its aim
And squeezes slowly. With a shriek of fright
I fall forever from the cliffs of blame.

Watching my body vanish, I awake
To hear the sounds I never thought to make.

III. UNDER PROTECTION

One side wet and one side dry,
My skin walls out the world.
I am blockaded, only barely in touch.
Life stiffens and keeps its distance.

I coast in tides of light and cold
Past knife-edge noises and the smoke of cities.
The daily lives that shoulder the sound of my name
Seethe distantly across the flats of time.

I have dreamed myself into the streets
Of a village on market day. Aloft on the battlements
I command the town, and prepare to seize
The contraband bartered by the peddlers.

Boots dazzling, muscles like halyards,
My subordinates stand tiptoe in their barrack,
Braced at unblinking armed attention
For the clang of the summons to suppress disorder.

Out there the life could be just anyone's,
But it happens to be mine.
And do I govern it, pay taxes on it?
No, it is mine, but it offers me no friendship.
It surrounds me.

IV. THE FLOWER OF SLEEP

When danger strips the mind
And slithers toward my throat,
I slink away in hopes to stay
Alive, aloft, afloat.

I cringe from the land of light
To bury myself in sleep
As though a sea surrounded me
Of endless dark and deep.

There dreamers hand me flowers,
Presuming me to be dead.
"No reason why he'd choose to lie
Asleep in a death-bed."

In this cradle of desperate rest
I snore away all fear—
The toppling tree, the storm at sea,
The Goddess striding near.

Such sleep does more than dream,
For when the sounds of day
Bring life to sight, I welcome light
To shudder my fear away.

But lately I dream of sleep,
Of wrecks and falling trees,
Of flowers laced around my waist
And grappling at my knees.

V. THE PUBLIC GARDEN

1.

This public park and I are strangers.
Look at it; sit on its benches; no matter.
It sleeps though I am agog in its presence.

2.

My turn to sleep. The park enters my privacy.
It wakes trembling in the spaces of my skull.
Its dry bones burst, its benches are my lovers.

3.

Each day the avenues I roam at night
Shut down when I awake, and no pretense
Of sleep will penetrate their spaces.
The visiting hours are over in the garden.

VI. THE VISITANT

You make yourself known to me in surprising places:
A laundry or a bus, or late at my office desk
After the others have gone, or where I listen
To an unspoiled voice read out a familiar poem.

Distracted, clouded over, I am startled
Awake by your presence stealing up behind me
To draw my breath and raise your hands and clasp
The soft familiar palms over my eyes.

VII. PRETENDING TO BE AWAKE

I am disgusted by the earthworks of my protection.
The clothes stink that curtain my nakedness
And beneath the wool my flesh is beginning to fester.
I must tease my life awake that now lies sleeping.

Others stay awake in the dark by laceration,
By thrashing out at workers, lovers, children,
To keep their ears alert to the sound of sorrow.
Some plunge into the tolerance of women
Or paralyze the tendrils of their brains
Desiring visions beyond sleep or waking.

If I could tempt this sleeping life awake!
It shuns me now that sometime did me seek.

VIII. THE COST OF PRETENDING

I would despise myself if I had the strength for it,
Would welcome the knife slitting the skin of my neck
As long as it did not falter and pour the blood.
Give me your hand, put it beneath my arm
Which closes on it, next to my heart. What
Do you hear of me? A steady beat, dull, leaden,
Irreversible. One who survives everything
Will shortly survive even himself.

IX. THE VOICES

I know those voices. They are all mine.
Tuesday the infant,
Wednesday the child,
Thursday the grown man wheedling
In rut or yearning in prayer,
Friday the sexless ancient, dreaming of sex.

Through the country of sleep
The voice of my blood
Trickles like water over limestone ledges.
Tributaries borrow its *bel canto*
To stage-whisper their way through dreams
Or heroize the arias of nightmare.

The voice is me, whatever voice or stream,
The voice of history rising through my sources.

X. FIRST VOICE: THE CHILD

Strange feet upon the stairs
Turn and walk this way.
I clothe myself in sleep
By shutting off my light.
They will not find the scent
Of hate on me tonight.

With one huge sigh, my chest
Moves easy, at the rate
Of every thief who breathes
More slowly than his guilt.
The door creaks open, but
My face, disguised in sleep,
Sings children's choruses.

The door has shut. The steps
Give way, descend the stairs.
The light, the book, emerge
From hiding. Like a bear
In blankets, all alert
For footsteps to ascend,
I lurk here in my lair.
They come? Then I'll pretend
Again to be asleep.

XI. SECOND VOICE: THE YOUTH

What wakened me? Moon?
Rustle of willows?
A cry or creaking stair?
Or was it shadows
Troubling my sleep
With a tug at my pillows?

Out of the shadows
Where sleep had been hiding
An ominous parcel
Comes quietly sliding—
Charred bones and ashes
On the tide riding.

Who could the parent be
Of this delivery?
Hands cold as serpents
Fumble the frippery,
Wrench at the wrapping,
Pause and lie quivering.

No, let it lie there
Inside its adorning.
Now should I stand to arms
After such warning,
Or pace the aisles of night
Until morning?

XII. THIRD VOICE: THE WIDOWER

The world has spread the word
That I am unworthy of it,
Crouching in lairs and caves
Pretending to be asleep.

First of the warnings: Love
Opened her eyes to me,
Then stopped her breath. No more
Pretending to be asleep.

Next came attentions, lavished
By divorcees and widows.
Though I took their bodies, mine
Pretended to be asleep.

Then came the nights, each darker
Than the one before. By night
I had no part to play.
By day I seemed asleep.

I know the sun by name.
This darkness may give ground
If I dream my way awake,
Pretending to be asleep.

XIII. FOURTH VOICE: THE GRANDMOTHER

I am an old woman living in a house beset with men.
It has been years since I heard a child
singing to itself.

These little men of mine are so little mine.
They live in the same dwelling but at a terrible distance.
They bring me their flowers but never notice me.
They wrestle with themselves,
with each other, father and son,
at all hours. I carry them platters of food.
They eat. They think themselves to be alone.
They walk like crustaceans.

There is no way for me to say, "Awake."
I must go on forever, smiling, serving, alert
for the accident of their waking.

Once young men stirred out of sleep
and smiled to find me naked beside them.
They gave me the flower of themselves,
the flower of their dream.
My little men do not yet know
they have been presented flowers.
They cannot recognize the face of the beloved
in their dream. How can they know,
unless they wake, that they have only
been pretending to be asleep?

XIV. POSSESSION

Inside me lives someone who writes poems,
Someone who has no words but from time to time
Borrows my words, whirls them through the dance
Of his purposes, then returns them.

My only evidence for his existence
Comes when I find poems on my desk
Ready for me to revise.
                    When did this happen?

Though I have never known who scribbled them
In secret, still I know my job.
I find them ready and waiting, I take over.
Possession they say is nine points in the poem.

III

THE YEARS

"*Ah, No. The years, the years.*
Down their carved names the raindrop ploughs."

THOMAS HARDY

OLD PHOTOGRAPH

Eight years dead, and dying
Many months before that, you leave me
No trace of yourself, except
These yellowing prints and some letters.
What do we know of the dead?
The needle of memory scratches
In the effort to remember.

Everything has been taken care of,
The papers are filed,
Most of the photographs mislaid
In a cigar-box.
Only this propped-up pose remains,
Rigid on the mantel in pious memory.

While you were dying I shuddered
At every jolt of pain that shot through you,
Watched as you speechlessly
Contorted with a numb tongue
To speak of your dying.
I was told I would forget that
And retain the memory of you
In the sounds of your husky laughter,
Your charm in company,
The glee you took in never
Saying goodbye on the telephone.

It isn't true. "True feeling
Leaves no memory," as Stendhal said.
It has left me nothing of you
But reminders that remind me of nothing.
Besides, only grief, sleeplessness,
Infant despair, betrayal.

These are you. I know nothing else
About you any more. I live behind glass,
Framed as tightly as your picture,
As frozen, as rigid, as blind.
How can I keep in touch
When there is nothing to touch?

September 23, 1967

BROTHERLY LOVE

My first and milktooth madam,
You walk in every woman,
Tinting her with the haze
And fever of the nursery.

I cracked you in my arms
Before I knew their uses
And sucked the brine of sex
At the blue moons of your bruises.

Outmaneuvered by wave
On wave of skirmishers,
You bear my scars as keepsakes
From foot to forelock.

At the far end of the row
My mind has hung your portrait.
It sees you thin and thirsty,
Then plump and pink and suckling,

Responsive as a mistress—
Whilst, unobserved, the certain
Secret hands of the hangman
Prepare themselves for business.

WORDS FOR MY FATHER

If God chooses you to have a son, tremble:
For just twelve years you may remain his father.
From twelve to twenty, try to be his teacher.
Thereafter you may hope to die his friend.

A MEXICAN VILLAGER

1. VOICE

Your gorgeous voice soared
down the flumes
of the tumbling canyons.
Sentences and judgments rang out
with the clarity of air that knows little rain.
Giver, trainer of tongues,
even cottonwoods do not grow without water.
Your voice's notes were poetry, pity, war.
It restored bodies to the dead.
It taunted my mother, turning you into her child.
It sharpened the duellers' blades of long-forgotten rages.
It yearned for the doting and the pity of your children.

2. VOYAGE

I, Telemachus, came to the sea after twenty years
and sailed to inquire
through all the trafficked harbors of the world
for news of my father's victories.
The voyage brought home little but pain,
messages garbled in transmission.
The air was dry and silent still.
My father's eyes turned away
from the knowledge-swollen face of his son.

3. DEAD

Later, when death began paying
its visits,
we were manacled by the knowledge
of how Penelope, infuriatingly patient,
had bound us together.
On the voyages since, another ten years,
we have kept silence like Greeks
"carrying heavy urns full of the ashes of our ancestors."
More men and women have died.
We have not forgotten
your mother's rectitude, her shabby flirtatious plumage,
nor your father, whose testament
was leaner than you desired—as every father's is.
His blood has scalded you
but you need not share his blame.
Give him your blessing.

4. ROAD

I walk forward in the afternoon of dying
along the road of words, cruel to the feet.
The dry tawny hills below your orchard
stretch away without shade or the sound of water.
Not yet in sight of you, Laertes, I hear your
cough, your parched and grating throat.
Shall I answer the question you are sure to ask?
If you are Odysseus, my son, come back,
Give me some proof, a sign to make me sure.
I have three signs: the scar, the trees, the words.
The scar of our parting, which has never healed.
The trees you planted, felled, buried under rubble.
The love we shared, carried by words only.
Deeds overwhelmed us.

5. WORDS

Words need not always fail.
No matter how seldom
we gather ourselves
to gather our hopes
into flocks, herding them before us
to huddle in their pens,
they are our dearest gift from this sparse soil,
the locked and grudging earth. They are
our servants, our sacrifice, our pledges.

Your gift to me
is my gift to you.

FOUR LOVE POEMS

I. FOR A DANCER

You cantered like a colt across the moon,
Fawned gratefully upon a lover's breast,
Scaled waterfalls, rang changes on the tune
Of love for beasts in caves. Gorgeously dressed,
You stalked in pride, a magical conceit,
Through woods with spirits in them, where you changed
Destruction to delight. Each of your feet
Was a perfect bird at the end of its bough arranged.

Transformed by sleep one day, you found you slept:
Your limbs were lead, could make no move. Desire
Became a wingless falcon, and you crept
In dream through palaces destroyed by fire.
Now music calls your name. A darkening glance
Of terror tells the dancer from the dance.

II. MAY WEEK 1950

You saw me first on the grass by the river and blushed,
Your body golden from all the blood it carried.
Weeks afterward, what luck, we rode a bus
Far across London to "The Prospect of Whitby,"
But stunned by the clink and roar we stole away
Over the hills and far away.

We were swept out into a beggar's opera.
Hands tiptoed to keep our secret meetings.
Half the half year's night was squandered
In seeking a bed to let our bodies breathe,
A city pasture for our lips and hands
That so teased you and so pleased you
What you did I must have done.

III. LENDING HANDS

Eyes swimming, she shakes out her hair—
What a tangled hedge it is
To mask her cheek against the air!

Lets her housemaid fingers brush
Where it hangs unshaken.
All else fails. I give a hand

To help her with her work. It works
Past the greeting of her face
To her neck and shoulders.

Hand, you are made welcome.
Neck bends to receive you.
Cloth stands aside at your entry.

Her right hand remembers your cunning
And warms you to your work
As her eager body's servant.

IV. THE LAST WORD

When I saw your head bow, I knew I had beaten you.
You shed no tears—not near me—but held your neck
Bare for the blow I had been too frightened
Ever to deliver, even in words. And now,
In spite of me, plummeting it came.
Frozen we both waited for its fall.

Most of what you gave me I have forgotten
With my mind but taken into my body,
But this I remember well: the bones of your neck
And the strain in my shoulders as I heaved up that huge
Double blade and snapped my wrists to swing
The handle down and hear the axe's edge
Nick through your flesh and creak into the block.

THE TWO OF YOU

I.

Your face is tense as wire within a wire
   When you consent to bed with sunlight flying.
The dervish flashes up into the fire.
   Not to be lost to love is to be dying.

Molten and greedy, quivering in my arms,
   You gnaw, you tear, you moan beneath my prying.
Our veins are full of sunlight as a field.
   Not to be lost to love is to be dying.

These fearful bodies rage against our will.
   (Our love is truth and leaves no room for lying.)
These stones, these walls, this house, this windowsill
   Are not to be lost. To love is to be dying.

II.

Outdoors the breeze blows childlike, notwithstanding
   Tomorrow it could be carrying sounds of war.
As we pass, we turn toward each other
   Like lovers in a bed.

We preserve house-plants, growing creatures,
   By constancy of warmth. In their season
Light airs are given entrance. We exclude only
   The brazen winds that turn flesh into stone.

Nourished by our senses and attentions
   This house will open up into a palace
Where children dress themselves in royal robes
   And swagger with the certainty of angels.

To hear one another's voices without speaking
　　　Composes the music of this house. The time
Of storms is welcomed as a penance.
　　　This house is silent and fragile as God.

CALYPSO

She found him facing out into the fog
At the edge of the sea, stooping, winnowing
Stones with all the care of the demented,
Hurling them into the murk, low along
The surface, skipping them like petrels.
He wandered by the shore, halting and stooping,
Leaning abruptly for additional
Hates to send spinning out to sea.
She watched from the cliff over his restlessness
And ached to hold him in her arms—held
Herself away from him, for an embrace
Would only remind his body of its bruises.
Hobbling a step, stooping, sorting the stones,
Hurling them again, as though he hoped
To force them, slippery beneath the sea,
To draw him after them, he threw and threw.
The shore wind whipped the bracken by the path,
Pressed out against the fog which yielded to it
And took it in and closed and gave no ground.
A woman could do nothing for him now,
Though she had known for months that this was coming—
Long before he guessed, even before
She herself could have put it into words—
His occupation gone, his enterprise swallowed.
The tide was out, the stones lay high and dry.
Terns chirruped in the fog along the shore.
The fog pressed on the land a little closer
And she could scarcely see him now, while he
Would never look back to where she stood behind him,
Just as he would never know that she
Had watched him strive, delude himself, and fail,
Had known all his evasions and deceits,
His minor infidelities, his hopes

That this time shabbiness would go unnoticed.
The only way to show her love for him
Was learning how to stand unseen
Until he chose to notice her—to laugh
Or storm or touch her breast or ask for food
And, though she was invisible, to smile for her.
Now in the fog he'd wandered farther off
Than she had ever lost him, yet she still
Was more aware of him and his despair
Than fog and sea and wind and stones together.
And so she turned, knowing herself helpless,
Leaving her man to men's devices, and the wind
Struck at her face as she walked weeping home.

STUMPS

The field is studded with their thousand lives.
All that is left of all that tracery
Pokes through the goldenrod in amputations
Too short to see, too tall to be mown over.
Their knuckles sprout new fingers every April.
I go my rounds in August trimming them back.
The roots, now elderly, are just as far
Involved in growing as they ever were,
But their suckers are sickly and cannot survive
Unless they're given help by God or me.

After a year or two of this flirtation
I snap trees off by hand which saw and axe
Once needed all their edges to bring down.
Poison could lull these lives to a merciful end,
But I as owner claim the dark indulgence
Of giving them a chance to sprout once more.
Crops like mine are not so much planted as buried.

PETER DAVISON

Peter Davison was born in 1928 in New York
City, raised in Colorado, educated at
Harvard College and Cambridge University.
His father is the poet Edward Davison. He
has published two earlier books of poems:
The Breaking of the Day (the 1964 volume in
the Yale Series of Younger Poets) and *The
City and the Island* (1966). He is Director of the
Atlantic Monthly Press in Boston and lives in
Cambridge with his wife, son, and daughter.